HOW TO DE-ESCALATE CONFLICTS USING BEHAVIORAL SCIENCE

A Humanist Learning Systems Companion Book

By Jennifer Hancock

Edited by, Reginald V. Finley Sr

I0510198

Copyright 2018 by Jennifer Hancock
Published 2018 by Jennifer Hancock
CreateSpace Edition
ISBN-13: 978-1717305770
ISBN-10: 1717305776

Title: How to De-Escalate Conflicts Using
Behavioral Science
Author: Jennifer Hancock
Edited: Reginald V. Finley Sr

This book is also available in print at most online
retailers and as an audiobook

Table of Contents

CHAPTER 1: INTRODUCTION: WHY THIS BOOK?

This is the companion book to the online course *How to De-Escalate Conflicts Using Behavioral Science*. This book will help you learn how to use behavioral science to respond to conflict and other interpersonal problems in a way that will actually fix the problem. It will help you learn how to stand your ground while still being compassionate and avoid getting drawn into other people's drama.

This book will help you learn a science-based approach to conflict resolution and help you understand how compassion can help resolve workplace behavior issues. Being able to reinforce organizational core values by modeling respectful conflict resolution behavior in difficult situations is an added bonus.

Individuals and groups can benefit from this course. For more information on this course visit: https://humanistlearning.com/de-escalate-conflicts/

This book contains transcripts of the course for easy home reference.

Why Behavioral Science?

Can behavioral science help us learn how to respond to conflict so we can be happier and more effectively help solve our problems without getting drawn into unnecessary drama? Yes it can... and

Jennifer Hancock, the author of several award winning books and founder of Humanist Learning Systems, will teach us how. She specializes in humanistic management and programs focused on how to stop bullying and harassment using science. Her insights on how to combine philosophy and science to help solve our problems more effectively have helped countless people all over the world.

This program and book is based on behavioral psychology and discusses how your responses impact other people so that you can choose a response that will help you stand your ground while still being compassionate about the problem that needs to be solved. The goal of this program is to help you learn how to use the science of behavior to respond professionally even in situations where the people around you are freaking out.

~~~~~

CHAPTER 2: TYPES OF CONFLICTS

Conflict is defined as: *a serious disagreement or argument, typically a protracted one.*

People disagree all of the time; usually, we can resolve those disagreements. The difficulty arises when we can't resolve those disagreements, or when the disagreement becomes protracted and starts interfering with other aspects of the relationship. This, is when we start to call it, a conflict.

There are 4 basic types of conflicts.

Interpersonal – where 2 people disagree to the point of conflict.

Intrapersonal – within a single individual. When you are wrestling with some conflict in your thinking and are unable to resolve it.

Intragroup – a conflict within a team where multiple people are in conflict or taking sides in an interpersonal conflict, which then infects the entire group

And **Intergroup** – when there is a conflict between different groups – say between your sales team and your maintenance team.

A conflict is a disagreement that becomes protracted to the point of inaction. The disagreement stops being a disagreement – ie: something rational we can talk about and work out. And starts becoming personal.

~~~~~

CHAPTER 3: RATIONAL DISCUSSION VS. IRRATIONAL CONFLICT

In order to understand how to use behavioral science to help us resolve conflicts, we first need to recognize that not all conflicts are rational.

If they have progressed to the conflict stage, what is happening is probably anything but rational.

One of the reasons what is happening is irrational is because when we are in conflict, we tend to think tribally. We view people who are different and who disagree with us as "other". This can happen for many reasons. Maybe we just do not like the other person or groups of people, so we label them "other." Perhaps we just respond negatively to the suggestions of the other person. Or, maybe, we don't respect that person at all... if we ever did. It could be that when we don't get our way, we revert to tribal thinking.

Tribal thinking is instinctual. It's the non-conscious assumption that our tribe is safe and good; whereas, the other tribe is dangerous and scary. We all do this. It is hard wired into our brain and we have to actively work around our tendency to label people as "other."

It is easy to see why tribal thinking interferes with disagreements and conflicts. If they don't agree with us, they must be other – ie: not in our tribe.

When we label someone as "other" and our tribal instincts kick in, we don't view them as fully human. So we don't respect them as we do members of our tribe. They are "other" and we view them and everything they do as suspicious.

The other problem is when tribal instincts kick in, a moral dynamic starts playing out. We believe our tribe or team is good and the other is bad. This is evolutionary thinking. It's instinctual and very hard to combat. The result though, is not just a lack of respect for those deemed to be other, but a view that the other is immoral and that fighting them is therefore "just."

For obvious reasons, this is really problematic in a work environment. First, it makes resolving the conflict very hard to do; and second, since everyone is working for the same company, everyone should be on the same team or tribe even if they are in different working groups.

Sometimes, the conflicts arise from insecurity. If one person doesn't feel respected, they will often project that lack of respect onto others and then their tribal instincts kick in and exacerbate the problem.

The common theme in all of this is a lack of respect. This lack of respect can be either perceived or actual, along with the view that the other person is "other" (in a tribal and therefore moral sense).

This is why most conflict management programs or techniques involve helping the parties involved in the conflict move past their instinctual tribal thinking to bring the "other" into the tribe of those we view and treat with respect.

Until that happens, you won't be able to resolve the conflict.

This is why Humanism is so critical to management functions. Humanism helps us see "others", including others who are complete and total jerks, as fully human, part of our tribe, and therefore worthy of basic levels of respect.

Humanism helps us overcome our tribal thinking and insecurities so that we can see the other person for who they really are, and not who our insecure tribal brain is trying to convince us they are just to protect our own fragile egos.

My point is that conflict is rarely rational and we need to recognize how these instinctual fears and biases impact our thinking and how these flaws in our thinking manifest as conflict.

They usually manifest in conflict as a perceived lack of respect, which is self fulfilling and – contagious – meaning – if you disrespect someone, they are probably going to return the favor and disrespect you.

It also manifests as an unwillingness to listen to a rational argument. The other person is evil and/or insane so I don't have to listen to what they are arguing because – whatever it is – it is evil or insane. We have all thought this way. I certainly have. More than likely, you have been the victim of someone thinking about you this way. This occurs quite often in politics.

This isn't simply about a lack of respect, it's a disconnect that our brains do to protect us from new information that may conflict with our worldview and our ego.

People devolve into conflict because they are trying to protect themselves in some way.

The question is, "How do we help ourselves and others move past our insecurities and tribal instincts so that we can start moving ourselves out of 'conflict' mode and into rational disagreement mode?"

~~~~~

CHAPTER 4: BEHAVIOR MATTERS

The answer to how do we move out of conflict mode into rational disagreement mode is that – behavior matters.

Conflicts are a problem for 2 reasons:

1.) First and foremost – they are preventing problems from being solved and

2.) They usually manifest in the workplace as inappropriate behavior.

This is a behavior problem. If you fix the behavior, you can fix the problem.

Disrespect:

Disrespect is at the heart of conflict and disrespect manifests in a myriad of ways.

Sometimes people behave passive aggressively. Maybe they don't invite the person they are in conflict with to an important meeting. Or maybe they spread rumors about them. Or maybe they just talk crap about them and try to rally support for their side and against the other person. Maybe they withhold information, or set someone up for failure. Or they compete aggressively.

Sometimes this "competition" manifests as bullying, harassment, and denigration as a way for the "competitor" to win and the other person to lose.

Regardless of HOW it manifests, it's not only unprofessional, it's harming your work; because, if you can't resolve problems rationally, your company has a problem.

If someone is responding to rational disagreement by engaging in irrational conflict, then your first goal is to stop their irrational behavior so that they can start engaging their brain and be more rational.

When people take what should have been a rational disagreement and engage in inappropriate conflict behavior as a way to deal with the disagreement – which of course, doesn't resolve the disagreement – all they are doing is making it worse.

To resolve the conflict, we have to change the behavior so that we can address the disagreement at the root of the conflict.

And … if there wasn't a disagreement, and the bad behavior is just that, bad behavior, we need to get it to stop, regardless. So that's where we need to focus our energy.

CHAPTER 5: USING SCIENCE TO "TWEAK" BEHAVIOR

If we want to de-escalate conflicts, we have to stop the bad behavior that defines the conflict.

Whether it is someone yelling, or passive aggressive withholding of information, social exclusion or even physical intimidation, we have a behavior that is inappropriate and preventing resolution from occurring.

To de-escalate, we need to decrease or eliminate whatever the unwanted behavior is. The good news is that behavioral psychologists have known how to stop and eliminate unwanted behavior for decades now. It's a technique called – extinguishing a behavior.

The way it works is that you don't reinforce the behavior you want to eliminate.

Yep, That's it.

You don't punish. You don't get angry. You don't get sad. You just … eliminate the reward.

Like all simple things, it's anything but simple to do in real life.

It's not always clear what the reward for a behavior is. It isn't always clear how *we* are feeding a behavior that we don't want in someone else. This is about taking responsibility for our own behavior first and foremost, and most people don't want to do that.

There is also some trickiness to this because, even if you manage to eliminate the reward, all you have really done is start the "behavioral extinction" process.

The hard part is continuing to eliminate the reward when the person behaving badly tries other clever ways to get their way.

Think about it like this:

A person is behaving badly because – it works for them in some way. Maybe if they throw a tantrum, they get their way. Suddenly – they don't get their way. What do they do? Like all children, they attempt to tantrum harder.

To people who don't understand the science, it seems like removing the reward didn't work. It actually did. It just takes repetition and consistency over time to get them to stop. Just like it does for kids.

The point is – if you are going to de-escalate a conflict, you have to pay attention to how you respond to the other person and tweak your own behavior so that you no longer reward their bad behavior inadvertently.

~~~~~

CHAPTER 6: UNDERSTANDING YOUR RESPONSE

Interpersonal interactions are like a dance. Person 1 does something and person 2 responds. Person 1 responds to what person 2 does and they trade responses back and forth. It's an interaction.

In the case of an interpersonal conflict, you are usually responding to the antagonistic behavior of the other person. They are then responding to how you responded to them and the cycle continues. Our goal is to use science to break that cycle.

Understanding that your response will have an impact on how the other person responds is the key to interpersonal enlightenment! You, despite all your triggers, have the ability to choose how you respond!

That's great news. The problem is – what sort of response is going to help a cantankerous cranky person, be less … combative?

The answer is, in general, is that a neutral polite response will. There are some caveats with respect to violence that could be mentioned but this goes beyond the scope of this work. Generally, a neutral polite response is not a good response to physical violence. For now – let's assume you aren't being physically attacked and you can respond to whatever is happening verbally.

Let's dive into the science first and then talk about how we use this information in reality.

Type of Responses:

There are three types of possible responses. (Please note that if you took psychology, I will be using these terms incorrectly – I do that on purpose to focus on terms a lay person can understand).

Positive Reinforcement– where you do something the other person likes and it therefore reinforces the behavior.

Negative Reinforcement – where you do something the other person doesn't like, and inadvertently reinforce the behavior.

Neutral Response – where what you did wasn't good or bad for the other person. It's just – neutral

When we deal with people who are difficult, we tend to respond …. Negatively. That's to be expected. We may get cranky in return. We may decide we don't want to deal with them and get passive aggressive. We may try to pretend to be nice all the while thinking negative horrid thoughts and then are surprised when the person picks up on that despite us pretending to be nice. (Yes we all do it, and it never works!)

What you need to understand is that from a behavioral conditioning perspective – negative reinforcement is still reinforcement. It actually makes bad cranky behavior worse!

This is pretty obvious. Fighting cranky stupidity with cranky stupidity is pretty stupid. All that the cranky person learns from you being cranky back is that their crankiness was totally justified.

A Counterintuitive Approach

What's counterintuitive is that being nice doesn't work either.

We've all had the experience, where someone is nasty to us, and we respond by being genuinely nice and they lash out at us. There is a reason for that. And that is that positive reinforcement is also reinforcement. Basically, when you are nice, what you are teaching the cranky obnoxious person is that if I am cranky and obnoxious, people are nice to me. And, that means they will do it more because – being cranky and combative worked!!!

The best response to a combative cranky person is an emotionally neutral response. In order to get people to stop behaving badly, you have to stop rewarding them for behaving badly. I'm not saying don't be nice to them. I'm saying, be nice to them when they are nice to you, but don't be mean to them either!!!!

What you want to do is not reward their inappropriate behavior, while still engaging with the person politely. What you have to do is not respond to the cranky and redirect towards a positive interaction (which you can then positively respond to).

For instance:
Say you have a frazzled co-worker who is frantic and blaming you for the fact that you can't turn around their request in the time they want. And … their anger at you is misplaced because it's their fault for not coming to you sooner or giving themselves enough lead time to get the project done right. They are yelling at you! What do you do?

You could yell back. That would be negative and that's pretty much how conflicts spiral out of control.

You could apologize and do your best. That would be the positive response. But all you've taught them is that being visibly angry with you is the best way to bully you into doing work you either shouldn't be doing or at a level of quality that isn't up to your standards or in a way that will lead to further abuse. That's not good either.

Your third option is to remain calm (a neutral response). Sympathize with their plight. Understand that when they yell at you, they are doing so because they can't really yell at themselves. Don't get baited into their drama. This is their problem, not yours and if they want you to help them, they have to be calm and allow you to help them.

Notice the focus. You are willing to help – if they will let you help them!!! As long as they are being cranky, cantankerous and ornery – they aren't allowing you to help them.

To pull this off, don't get frazzled. Stand your ground politely and calmly with as little emotion as you can muster, say something along the lines of:

"I'm sorry Dave, but I can't do that."

"I understand you are under a deadline (or whatever else the problem is), but what you want can't be done because of whatever the reason is. I'm sorry, but perhaps we can solve your problem another way."

I know you are now all thinking – if I did this – the other person would go ballistic. And they probably will. Like I said – this – just starts the process. If that happens, don't argue with them. Unless they calm down and behave professionally, don't reward their cranky combative behavior. Just keep repeating – "I'm sorry Dave, but I can't do that – perhaps we can solve your problem another way."

Notice that this is calm. It's sympathetic, it's helpful. But … you didn't solve their problem for them. In fact, you refused to solve their problem for them until they calmed down and behaved professionally. But you did so in a way that makes it so they can't accuse you of being unhelpful.

What you did is ask them calmly if they want you to help solve their current problem. It doesn't really matter what you say as long as it is: a.) factual, and b.) is said calmly and opens the door to problem solving.

If they don't want you to solve their problem because all they want to do is rant – great! Don't waste your time trying to solve that problem, it's not a problem you can solve, except to listen. If that's where they are – just keep repeating your calm – I understand, but … do you want me to help you? Statement.

Only try to solve their problem if they ask you to. Nicely! If they do, great – NOW you can have a rational discussion about the best way to solve the problem. You can suggest alternatives, or compromises. Perhaps if we didn't do this, but did this instead – you could still get this out on time.

As long as they are emotionally agitated, you can't have a rational discussion. Stay calm if they are frantic. Slow down – deliberately. Counter their cranky franticness with calm deliberateness. You are modeling the emotional state you want them to get to. Which is calm and rational so that you can problem-solve instead of argue.

Yes – this is a lot like helping a kid with a tantrum. In fact, it's everything like helping a kid cope with a tantrum. Same dynamic – same science. You remain calm and encourage them to be calm as well.

If they can't calm down, that's fine. Sympathize with their anxiety and let them know that you will help them however you can, within the constraints that exist and that they should call you when they are ready to discuss realistic alternatives.

For example: I used to do GIS work for a tower company. My boss would ask me to do a project. He would give me a time frame. If it wasn't realistic, I would laugh and say – no really, when do you need this done by and we would discuss his real needs and what was realistic for me to do and how long it would realistically take. If I had buckled and said ok to an unrealistic time frame I would have been doing him and myself and the company a disservice. I was there to help, but I could only help by being honest and doing so in a way that encouraged rational problem solving.

Remain calm and don't be bullied into doing something you know is wrong or commit to doing something that can't be done or shouldn't be done in the way they want it done.

In my experience, the people who were the crankiest with me often turn into my greatest supporters because I help them help themselves solve their problems, by encouraging them to calmly and rationally solve their problems.

I don't enter into a conflict with them. I support them in a way that forces them to respect me. I help them overcome their crankiness to get to a solution that actually works. And, I trained them to be nice and professional with me, otherwise they aren't getting diddly squat.

~~~~~

CHAPTER 7: DON'T GET DRAWN INTO THE DRAMA

Remaining calm and trying to refocus on problem solving isn't easy to do. In fact, it's often very very hard. Both you and the person you are finding yourself in conflict with, have been conditioned throughout the course of your life. You have your own set of triggers and weird behaviors that you don't control well.

You have your own limitations in terms of mental health functioning, physical health issues that affect your mental health and an entire lifetime of facing a world that isn't always nice to you. We all have scars and we are all sensitive. Some of us more than others.

When you take someone who is suffering and spreading their suffering around through general crankiness and add them to your suffering, it's not a good combination.

How do you create boundaries and not get drawn into their drama and not allow their bad behavior to trigger your bad behavior?

First, understand, their bad behavior isn't about you even if it is directed at you! You have no idea why this person is behaving this way and that's ok. You don't need to. You just have to accept that they are behaving unprofessionally. They are cranky and combative with us. We don't want them to be. Because it makes us feel bad or it triggers our insecurities in some way. All we know is THEY need to stop – for us.

We cause ourselves an amazing amount of frustration by trying to make other people behave better for US. It's a futile thing to do. You can't change other people's behavior. Heck, most of us can't even change our own!

It Isn't About You

Understanding that their behavior isn't about you does two things for you: 1.) You stop making it about you and 2.) You stop trying to make them change.

If someone is cranky because there is a whole lot that has gone on in their lives, then it's silly to get mad at them for not being perfectly wonderful to you. That's about you. And as long as you are focused on how they are impacting you, you will be stuck in a fruitless loop of insecurity. Your insecurity feeding off of theirs and around and around you go.

If you accept – this is just who they are and you don't know why they are behaving this way, you won't get sucked into their drama! You stop trying to make them be better for your sake, and get on with dealing with them as they are as best you can. You can calmly offer to help without being sucked into the drama.

This little tweak – to how you think of these interactions – changes everything. The key to making this work is humility and compassion. Humility to know your own emotional limitations and stressors and your own tendencies towards defensive tribal thinking. And compassion to understand that others may be suffering and stressing too.

Whatever is causing this person to behave the way they are, they have their own stuff going on and they are responding to it as best they can. Give them some space and compassion.

~~~~~

CHAPTER 8: COMPASSION AS A TOOL

I find that the key to remaining calm and not allowing the other person to trigger me into joining them in a conflict, is to use compassion.

To me, compassion is a tool. It helps me see the situation more realistically. It helps me to remain calm so I can respond in a neutral way. And it helps me model the behavior I want and expect back from them.

Additionally, if someone is itching for a fight, and you don't fight them, they will eventually de-escalate because most people have no idea how to deal with an enemy who refuses to be an enemy. The challenge is to invoke your compassion for people who are being nasty to you. Intentionally.

I find that considering the other person as a flawed human who is behaving badly for some reason that has nothing to do with me helps. I imagine all sorts of scenarios where this other poor person is just damaged in some way I can't possibly fathom. Maybe they just lost a child, or they narrowly escaped an accident on the way to work. Perhaps they didn't get enough sleep.

I don't need to be right about why the other person is behaving badly. The purpose of this exercise is to activate my compassion for them so that: a) I consider them as part of my tribe worthy of respect, and b) so that instead of getting drawn into their drama, I respond in a calm and helpful mode instead of an angry and agitated - it's all about me mode.

The more I can do this, the more I will de-escalate potential conflicts and help resolve them before they even get started.

Feeling compassion for someone, makes sure I don't enter conflict mode with them. It helps me ground them as part of my tribe and reduces my tribal instincts so that I can consider what they are telling me rationally.

It helps me be in supportive problem solving mode with them without inadvertently reinforcing their bad behavior. I can wait them out until they calm down. And they almost always calm down because you would be a cad to refuse someone's help if they kept offering it.

Finally, IF it turns out that this isn't a conflict, that it's just someone who is bullying... this same compassionate strategy will help ensure that they learn – you can't be bullied into submission.

~~~~~

CHAPTER 9: AN EXAMPLE

I'm going to give you an example of a customer service rep dealing with a cranky customer in full fight mode.

I had to go to a car rental once. There was a guy at the counter in front of me and he was cranky... I mean, **REALLY** cranky. Why?

Well, he needed to re-rent the car that was rented to him. He had this car for a month because his car was in the shop and wasn't ready yet. He was upset that he had to fill out new paperwork. He didn't understand why it needed to be done. All of his information was in the computer, "Why do I have to sign the form again? Blah, blah, blah."

The clerk was polite and calm and didn't engage in a debate about the rules. He just said, "I understand, but … I need you to sign this form to extend the rental past one month."

He let the guy rant, rave and complain loudly while he calmly did the paperwork. He didn't get mad or flustered or upset. He didn't argue. He didn't get sucked into this guy's drama. He did the work that needed to be done; as professionally as he could and that was it. He did his job.

It was a perfect response because the guy wasn't actually mad at the clerk. He was mad at the dealership who hadn't fixed his car after a month of working on it which is why he was forced to have a rental car in the first place.

This guy's anger wasn't even directed at the right person!!

The staff could have gotten flustered; but, what good would that have done? Would it have helped the customer? No. Would it have helped the staff feel better? No. Would it have helped the other customers who were witnessing this angry man's performance? No.

Remaining calm and allowing this guy to vent while calmly solving his problem despite his crankiness at having the problem at all was the best response. After *cranky guy* left, I complimented the staff on doing an amazing job in the face of such negativity.

They just shrugged, it is what it is and the guy probably had a bad day. They did what they needed to do to help the guy solve his problem even if he wasn't appreciative. They didn't let the cranky guy get to them. They didn't fight or get drawn into his drama. They didn't insist he not be cranky. They just remained calm and did their job as best they could.

They solved the problem, but not in the way the guy wanted. He wasn't able to bully them into doing something they couldn't or shouldn't be doing. They did – however, solve the problem for this man in an extraordinarily professional way.

Does this work in interpersonal conflicts in a workplace? Yes. Because it's the same dynamic playing out. Someone is behaving badly, but behind that is a problem that needs to be solved.

Unfortunately, some people behave badly when under stress and then they take out their anger on people who don't deserve it. They then rationalize why they behaved badly and behave even more badly.

In a professional environment, when someone is behaving unprofessionally with you, the best thing you can do is double down on the calm polite professional demeanor and offer to help, just don't help until they ask for your help in a respectful compassionate way.

In most cases, when you remain calm and keep offering to help, most people will eventually calm down and work with you and the conflict will go away.

You have given them no reason to be mad at you and no reason to justify conflict with you. Most people will respect that. Most people, when you are respectful and helpful, will eventually reciprocate – once they calm down.

You Can't Fix Everyone
Some people won't calm down. That's ok. That's not on you. That's on them. By not fighting with

them, you help yourself by remaining professional in the face of sometimes really unpleasant and unprofessional behavior.

Their bad behavior is not a reflection on you even if it is directed at you. It's a reflection on them. All you can do is not feed their fire. It is frustrating to watch people dig their own holes, but sometimes, all you can do is calmly say – hey – there is a better way. If they don't take that better way. Feel bad for them, but don't join them in the hole.

~~~~~

CHAPTER 10: DON'T FAKE IT

One last thing I want to caution you on. Remaining calm is a skill that has to be practiced. Being calm is not something you can fake.

Most humans are really adept at reading body language and tone of voice. We understand the meaning and the emotional intent even if it isn't said out loud. You can't remain calm and emotionally neutral if you are thinking nasty horrible things about the cranky people you encounter. They will hear your nastiness come out. Seriously – they will. This is why you need to feel compassion for them.

Remember at the beginning I talked about why people are cranky and why people are combative, and why they devolve into conflict? I did that so that instead of you being cranky that the other person is cranky – you will feel compassion for them instead. Your compassion will help you respond to the person more authentically so that what you want them to hear is what they actually hear. You being calm despite their crankiness.

Feeling sorry for them will ensure that your communication with them isn't laced with malice, but with compassion and pity instead. And again, this isn't something you can fake. If you just can't respect someone, pity them instead and try to think of them compassionately. What you may just find is that when you stop treating them as if they are a threat to you or that you hate them, they will stop responding to you as if you are a threat who hates them!

Communication is a two-way street. If you hate someone, they will respond to that hate even if you don't say it out loud.

The best way to ensure your communication is as polite and respectful as you would like it to be is to feel compassion and to be responsible for your side of the conflict. Feeling compassion for someone requires you to respect them as humans first. Even if they are unbelievably cranky humans who are behaving horribly, compassion will help you authentically feel respect for them as an individual, even if you don't respect their behavior.

That respect will be heard and felt by the other person and it's the necessary first step to help de-escalate conflicts.

~~~~~

CHAPTER 11: RECAP

In order to de-escalate conflicts, you have to model respectful conflict resolution behavior. You do this by remaining calm and polite and professional and focus on problem solving.

Compassion for the other person, even if they are behaving badly will help you respond in the calm neutral way required to get the unwanted bad behavior to stop.

Even when you do everything right, it will still take time. Conflicts and communication problems don't develop overnight, and they take time to unwind. Just keep being calm, professional, polite, compassionate and helpful and the other person will eventually learn that the best way to work with you and get work out of you is to be calm, professional, polite, compassionate and helpful. The bonus is that you will be modeling and helping to establish a professional norm that is actually – professional.

Finally – don't become part of the problem. Anytime you find yourself feeling self-righteous, you are engaging in tribal thinking which means, you are part of the problem. Stop and adjust your attitude and frame of reference.

Stop making it about you and start responding in a neutral calm compassionate way. Once the other person is calm, engage in positive problem-solving.

~~~~~

CHAPTER 12: ABOUT THE AUTHOR:

 Jennifer Hancock is a mom, author of several books, and founder of Humanist Learning Systems. Jennifer is unique in that she was raised as a freethinker and is considered one of the top speakers and writers in the world of Humanism today. Her professional background is varied including stints in both the for profit and non-profit sectors. She has served as Director of Volunteer Services for the Los Angeles SPCA, sold international franchise licenses for a biotech firm, was the Manager of Acquisition Group Information for a ½ billion-dollar company and served as the executive director for the Humanists of Florida. When she became a mother, she decided to stay at home, but that didn't last long. Shortly after her son was born, she published her first book, *The Humanist Approach to Happiness: Practical Wisdom.* Her speaking and teaching business coalesced into the founding of Humanist Learning Systems which provides online personal and professional development training in humanistic business management and science-based harassment training that actually works.

More Learning from Jennifer Hancock

OTHER BOOKS BY JENNIFER HANCOCK

- The Humanist Approach to Happiness

- Jen Hancock's Handy Humanism Handbook

- The Bully Vaccine

- The Humanist Approach to Grief and Grieving

- How to Win Arguments Without Arguing

- Ending Harassment & Retaliation in the Workplace

- Why Bullies Bully & How to Stop Them Using Science

- Reality Based Decision Making for Effective Strategy Development

Courses taught by Jennifer Hancock

- Workplace Bullying for HR professionals

- Living Made Simpler

- An Introduction to Humanism

- Socratic Jujitsu: How to Win Arguments Without Argument

- Why Conflict Resolution Doesn't Work When the Problem is Bullying

- Bridging the Generational Divide: Millennials vs. Boomers

- Ending Harassment and Retaliation in the Workplace

- Reality Based Decision Making for Effective Strategy Development

- How to De-escalate Conflicts Using Behavioral Science

- Why is Change so Hard?

- Principles of Humanistic Management

- 7 Sins of Staff Management

- How to Handle Cranky Customer Problems

- New Manager Orientation

- Humanist Group Leadership Lessons

- Sexual harassment training that works – general

- Sexual harassment training that works – AB 1825

- Stop Bullying in our Workplace – Staff Training

- Sexual Harassment Compliance Training

- No Fear Act training

- Planning for Personal Success!

- Talking to your child about death

- The Bully Vaccine Toolkit

- How to talk to your child's school about bullying

- Why Bullies Bully & How to Stop Them

Connect with Me Online:

- Twitter:
  http://twitter.com/#!/JentheHumanist

- Facebook:
  http://www.facebook.com/JentheHuma
  nist

- Or sign up for my mailing list:
  http://eepurl.com/c3LuI

top

The End

###

www.ingramcontent.com/pod-product-compliance
Lightning Source LLC
Chambersburg PA
CBHW070518220526
45467CB00002B/732